The Trickster Riots

Poems by Taté Walker

Illustrated by Ohíya Walker

D1157506

ABALONE MOUNTAIN PRESS
A PLACE FOR INDIGENOUS WRITERS TO DISMANTLE THE CANON

For queer Indigenous youth.
You are enough and I love you.

-Taté Walker

To the kitchen table.
For bearing the weight
of 13 years of splattered paint.
(Look Ma, I'm a poet, too! And sorry about the mess.)

-Ohíya Walker

Contents

Contents, cont.

The Trickster Riots

the Lakota trickster
is called Iktómi
the spider

throughout history
Iktómi embodies useful
provocative roles
to teach lessons
obliterate cultural boundaries

The Trickster Riots
is a lyrical study of a wiŋyaŋ witkó
a Lakota Two Spirit
shedding the expectations
of performative Indigeneity

I am the trickster as rioter
furious and disaffected

I am the trickster as righter
libratic and ceremonial

And I am the trickster as writer
queer and full of story

Inspired by Teju Cole.

1

people say I walk
like I'm from the Big City

p u r p o s e f u l
and
u n f o r g i v i n g

unexpectedly light-footed
for someone my size
it's my strut
or maybe it's my resting stoic face
that says get out of my way
or I'll knock you out of my way
no, I'm not violent towards others
(I'm a Libra)

but I'm always prepared for violence
violence backed by medical science
by BMI BS
by scales and middle seats
by family and strangers alike
whose worry for my health
feels like a knife in the back
betrayals I know come in response to
this Body

they call me Thunder Thighs
a clichéd euphemism for fatass
they force to rhyme with badass
yet they never want to make
p h e n o m e n a l
t-shirts
that fit people over 2X
or put those people
people who look like me
on their vision boards

they tell me I'm not fat
like I haven't been here the whole time
they tell me I look great
as they cringe at their own insecurities
they say I'm so confident
scoffing at their own jiggly bits
disgusted by the parts of themselves
that remind them of
this Body

what they don't realize is
I am a raging prairie storm
called down with Wakíŋyaŋ
the Thunder Beings
to purge my landscape
of Western beauty standards

3

I rain down tears and sweat
released as a flood of unearned sins
s l o t h
and
g l u t t o n y
a twister collecting
too many books
too many tacos
and too many gym memberships
swollen with the weight of the
Weight Loss Industrial Complex
commodifying
this Body

my darkness seethes and expands
with every colonial ideal of airbrushed perfection
every judgmental stare from the next table over
every unsolicited piece of health advice
from nondoctors
and every actual doctor who thinks
the flu
depression
and a broken arm
are caused by fatness

every unflattering
unstriped
block-patterned
black garment
they fill fat-friendly clothing stores with
every chair designed to keep me
from sitting at the table
or next to you
and everything else in this too small world that
shrinks with each inch of awesome consumed with
this Body

the gusts gather to me like armor
whipping the winds of my name
through the air in a fierce caress
of electric potential
across this glorious body

t h u n d e r s t r u c k
explosions across my skin
leave trails of lighting
spiderwebs of physical memory
this body is a trickster
here be jagged strikes of teen trauma
shifting into communal spiritual sacrifices
and skins of protective motherhood

in my core lies
not two wolves
but Iktómi
a settler spider
gleefully whispering that
colonialism
sure does taste good to
this Body

so I keep feeding it
on days when I can stand free
of colonialism's web
these thighs rejoice and
redouble their efforts
to support the mass of stories and
love swelling inside

yes
these thighs have
chased off violence
locking tight in protection
but

these thighs also
open and dance
to the soft songs upon Ojibwe tongues
and these thighs remind me that together
we are responsible for releasing
the next generation of
formidable butterflies
upon the world
we are an Indigenous
magic
trick
coming together
his body and
this Body

I will not deflate
to fit into small spaces
and tiny minds
so I flash a smile
wear a crop top and short shorts
champion
these stretch marks
these thunder thighs
embrace these riotous trickster vibes
and know that today with every step
a booming chorus will
clap back at the world
with righteous gratitude for
this Body

+ + + +

I am a modern
Lakota wiŋyaŋ
no tipi
no paint
no feathers
I'm like no Indian
you've ever seen
because I am not
a blockbuster archetype

someone dressed like
a gothic taxidermist
is trying to sell me my own culture
in exchange for a cheap movie ticket
or all of my dignity
I get to see another actor in redface
broken English and all
good trade?

the worst part is
some Natives are so starved for attention that
many will take it in whatever form it's offered
when racism knocks on your door
it'll be riding a pinto
wearing a bird hat and
wrapped in a Comanche flag
and you just might adopt him
at least they spelled the tribe's name right

the actor says his goal was to
honor Natives with positive film representation
except that it's Tonto
except it's not a Native actor in a Native role
except they used white painter Kirby Sattler's
weirdly mystical painting "I Am Crow"
as inspiration for Tonto's costuming
Tonto means stupid in Spanish

why — WHY?!? — Tonto?
Cowboys and Indians was only fun to play
if you were actually always the cowboy
even after the game ended
besides, my people were too busy vanishing
into Edward Curtis' photographs
and boarding schools
to surround those wagons
only colonizers are nostalgic
for the Wild West

what's the big deal? you ask
while white kids ran around with fake headdresses and
plastic bows and arrows
being Indian in all the ways that counted
like access to and use of sacred sites and objects
and the freedom to worship and ceremony
was illegal until 1978
white irony is playing Indian
while actual Indians survive genocide

>you tell me I'm being too sensitive
>tell me to get over it
>tell me that it's just a movie
>that it's just a game
>it's just a costume, just a sports team
>a repurposed word, a fashion trend
>you feed me gourmet stereotypes
>seasoned with honorifics
>and everyone is invited to
>stuff themselves at this dinner party
>*our images are not our own*
>*they belong to those in power*

and I want to scream
THESE IMAGES HURT ME!
you may not know it
but they hurt you, too
no one wins when ours is a
Halloween heritage
DNA destiny
mascot manifestation
logo legacy
slot machine sovereignty
Tonto tradition
ancestry for the price of admission

FROM PTESÁŊWIŊ, WITH LOVE

I.

I'm 17 and it's my first time at sweat
men from the prison up the street sit in the dark
with us Native kids from the group home
no one has prepared me for what to expect
since I am supposed to come preloaded
with Ceremony 101

inside the lodge we're all hip to hip and too close
the smell of leather and dirt and b.o.
makes me thinks I've made another bad life choice
but mixed with wood smoke and sage
the air is an intoxicating blend of anxious prayer
and my barely-there spirit craves a fix

a Stygian darkness floods my eyes
sprinkled water kisses dozens of fired stones
and they create a passionate hiss of steam
it hits my exposed skin like a full-body slap
shocked, I gasp in air that burns my throat and lungs
a drum is struck to the rhythm of a Lakota prayer song
and both are loud enough
for our Milky Way ancestors to hear

my senses are overwhelmed with dread
deprived of emotion for so long
my body urges me to flee
from the pressure of all this feeling
but my mind
consumed by the darkest depression
welcomes the scorching heat
like my skin welcomes a razor blade
I feel a release coming
and I think this might be what dying feels like
trapped under a dome of panic and resignation
an eternity passes

II.

the medicine man ends the first round
he says without judgement we can leave
because ceremony is not a competition
the flap opens and a freezing February night sweeps in
to soothe and caress our seared bodies within
the breath I take feels new
like I haven't taken a real breath in a long time
my body prepares to escape exit
but one of the boys and two men depart
and I don't want out anymore

the flap closes and darkness returns
but it's not a crushing anxiety that covers me now
no—the obsidian staring back at me is comforting
a blanket over my head after a bad dream
the next round begins with a story about Ptesáŋwiŋ
White Buffalo Calf Woman
I'm pretty sure I know her
in the same sense I know math
she's important—universal
I just don't know why

this retelling is focused
not on Ptesáŋwiŋ's gifts
sacred directives and a sacred pipe
but instead on the respect she demands and is owed
the medicine man punctuates his tale
by offering cedar to the fired stones
my eyes take in the brief
sweet sparks just as hungrily
as my ears yearn for more of Ptesáŋwiŋ's story

with relish
and what I imagine is a shaming scowl toward the
lodge's men
and a conspirator's wink at me
the medicine man tells of how Ptesáŋwiŋ
strikes down the first man
to even *think* about taking advantage of her

the breath leaves my body all at once
and the stones haven't even been put to work yet
this round
like the sweltering steam yet to come
Ptesáŋwiŋ's tale saturates all available space
and I am again overwhelmed
not with dread
but with awe

violence against Native women
against me
was so normalized
so expected
to say I was awed by Ptesáŋwiŋ's story
is like saying a raindrop could fill an ocean
it's not enough

it surprised me that a man
a medicine man, sure, but a man, nonetheless
would choose to focus on a part of the story
usually told in the same way you'd speak of her hair or
eye color
just a detail
that impure thoughts
(*thoughts!*)
would render a wretch to naught but his bones
how many times in my life would I wish that upon a man

of all that's told in her story
this retribution
is often divulged as the implausible element
in most retellings
we're supposed to focus on her gifts
and the precise way we're to receive and practice them
not Ptesáŋwiŋ
and her intolerance for perversely unfocused men

but in this second round of sweat
the medicine man reminds us that Ptesáŋwiŋ
indeed all women and the consent they grant
are great gifts full of their own kind of ceremony

III.
I don't know that I was ever told
"women are sacred"
"you are sacred"
how do you tell that to a sexual abuse survivor
a mentally ill teenager
too often at the mercy of a man's whims
blamed for being in the wrong place at the wrong time
shamed for clothes I felt confident in
saying no too unconvincingly
not saying no enough
simultaneously gay-bashed and slut-shamed
if I'd done something different
it's my fault
sacred? do you mean scared?
if I am a gift
why haven't I been able to return myself
believe me, I've tried

Ptesáŋwiŋ tells us how to relate to one another
don't hurt women, the medicine man says
and he is speaking directly to the men at sweat
that is not our way
and it is not what Ptesáŋwiŋ taught us
don't beat on your women
don't rape them
don't kill them

though he is retelling Ptesáŋwiŋ's
Rules for Being a Good Relative™
this is the first time I'm hearing a man

tell another man
not to rape a woman
during the next round of sweat
some of the men cry as they pray to Tuŋkásila
for forgiveness
they have wronged many women
and they profess a wide range
of apologies and promises
but none of them give specifics

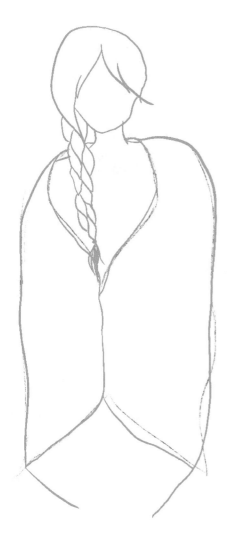

none of them say
"I won't speak out of turn"
"I will advocate for
        fair and equal pay"
"I will share housework
        and child-rearing
        responsibilities"
"I won't cause fear or harm
        as a way to exhibit
        power and dominance"
"I won't use words that
        demean or objectify
        women and Two Spirits"
"I won't excuse sexist
        behavior as a joke"
"I will ask for consent
        before touching another
        person or their property"
"I will expect these behaviors
        of other men"
So many ways to show respect
and accountability
left unrecognized
and perhaps unknown

IV.

20 years later
and men holding other men accountable
is just as unlikely
as a woman is to be armed
with a skeleton-revealing cloud
20 years later and I'm terrified
my own child
may end up on an #MMIR poster
Missing and Murdered Indigenous Relatives
just another red handprint
on the mouth of Indigenous women and Two Spirits
screaming to be
seen
heard
found

it's not an impossible task
to allow women and Two Spirits
to live without fear of violence
is it?
is it?
great men once
trusted
believed
ensistered
a strange woman
into a place of forever love
they can do it again

I have encountered Ptesáŋwiŋ many times
since that first inípi
she has emboldened my storytelling
not just what I tell others
but what I tell myself
the effort I once used to clench
my fists and jaw and body

tight against the world
I've slowly channeled into my heart
made it stronger
so it could hold all the amazing gifts
this life continues to bestow

I may not reveal the literal skeletons of evil men
but I've been known to battle toxic masculinity
and it helps to think that my work
to dismantle patriarchal oppression
in classrooms
media
and government systems
is not unlike what I imagine
Ptesáŋwiŋ was trying to do
all those years ago
bring the people back from the brink
not to simply survive
but to thrive

V.

I'm 17 and the final round of my first inípi has ended
the last of the drum's reverberations is gone
the flap opens and we exit
I am overwhelmed with jubilation
my heart has taken up the songs we've been singing
and my ears throb with strong, persistent beats
I crawl through the opening and think
this must be what birth feels like
hot and anointed with my own perspiration
toxins from another life cry out
steaming from every pore

I am a smudge
of warm hope
rising upward
tentatively offering
a prayer
for what I have been
given
this winter's night
a ceremony
a gift
a spark to light
the inevitable dark
days ahead

but darkness no longer
fills me with dread
though I am scared of
the unknowable journey
before me
I now also possess the
knowledge that
I am sacred
and I have
sacred things
to experience
and accomplish
gifts of my own
to share

I do not look back

SCISSORS OF COLONIALISM

there's a new poster on the walls
    of the Twitter Saloon
    WANTED: PRETENDIANS
    turn one in to the authenticity police
    and the reward is nothing
    short of short-term celeb-red-ty

exposing pretendians can be rewarding work
unmasking those cashing in on faux Indigeneity via
    $cholar$hip$
        keynote$
            $ocial media influencing
                and $pirituality $eminar$
demystifying the odd
fractional math of the Wannabe Tribe
    those clinging to family
    fairytales of royal lineages
unchecking the boxes of ladder-climbers
    who fetishize our cultural byproducts
    but dismiss our struggles and communities
side-eyeing those ancestry dot com results
    commodifying **Native American blood**
    into vampiric genetic markers
exposing pretendians is necessary—critical—to protect
sovereign people and nations

but some bounty hunters tracking pretendians
get overwhelmed
        they begin with sights set
        on accountability and harm reduction
        but soon seek the like-and-share thrill
        of public takedowns
        grossly attacking those relatives
        already existing in the margins
                Afro-Indigenous
                        and mixed Indigenous relatives
                                adopted relatives
                                        displaced urban relatives
                                                and those questioning
                                                the process

                        their tool of choice is a rusty
                        pair of scissors
                        found buried in the remnants of
                        boarding schools
                        a tool once used by
                                        the agents of colonialism
                                        to cut the braids off
                                        Indigenous children

                        neocolonialism has repurposed these
                        blades for today's gotcha markets
                        it urges Natives to slice
                        other Natives into **lists**
                                forming sharpened spreadsheets
                                that still work to sever us
                                from our cultural selves

scissor snicks reverberate throughout Indian Country
bounty hunters brandish these lists
        measuring sticks and DNA tests at the ready
        threatening anyone lacking federal recognition
        or a podcast

these self-appointed experts on Blood Quantum Mechanics
these enrollment vigilantes and identity gatekeepers
        flip through dubious research tactics
        performing 10s in journalism gymnastics
        and 0s in community healing

pretendians experience inconveniences
        actual Native people suffer injustices
colonized minds hear **ours** and think possession
        decolonized minds hear "ours" and feel connection
settlers say I have rights
        Indigenous people say *I have relatives*

yes
predators who exploit Indigeneity
        should be brought to justice
        not the kind served on the wild frontier
        of social media
        but the kind found in the hands
        of tribal knowledge keepers
we should trust the justice
        of auntological kinship practices

communities and cultures claimed
by suspected pretendians
        should decide
        whether to expose frauds or not
        and how
accessing familial bonds and ancestral memories
        can't be reckoned using colonial metrics

we are all connected
Mitákuye Oyásiŋ
    not by puppet strings
       or percentages
    but our responsibilities
       to each other
let's weaponize our identities
    against the state
not each other
    stop wrapping ourselves
       in scarcity
    begin recognizing ourselves
       with abundance

let's reimagine those scissors
    clipping colonialism's claws
    trimming the fat takers
    cutting lists into confetti
    shearing the shame of not-enoughness
       from our spirits
you and I can turn a tool of oppression and destruction
    into an instrument of love and creation

we've been here before:
white folks whoring
i'm sorry, **exploring**
brown territories

always expanding
never understanding
our declarations
of Indigenous affirmations

and like ships led astray
across waters of righteous
infestation
these pale people with
their
morally-flexible navigation
wash ashore and lay claim to our innovations
        lands
                bodies
                        ideas

white fear of being less
manifests as **it's mine**
while they evangelize the gospel
according to Capitalism

we've been here before:
white destinies shaped by
brown erasure
greener pastures await
on the other side of the racial divide
so we hide our kids, hide our wives
hide our lives
from the settler gazes that
don't see color

HERE
WE
ARE
NoW

we've been here before:
this desire for more
looks like
> **tricksy treaties**
> > **slippery pipelines**
> > > **gasping copper mines**
> > > > **and Sauvage parfume**

and white quellers silence
Indigenous critique while appropriating
everything
they never had to bleed for

white doublespeak is staying silent about
brown struggles
while disguising racist depictions
as First Amendment rights
wrapped in sports jerseys and sold as the latest
blockbusting
bestselling
window-dressed trend
no, that's not applause you hear
that's us trying to free ourselves from the
chains of your **good intentions**

we've been here before:
a white person gets rich off
Native images of yore
our images of now?
ignored

culture vultures circle overhead
uninspired
and looking to **exploit**
the pieces of our spirits
we were able to hold onto
in the face of genocide

27

we've been here before:
you get defensive
whine aggressively
about all the pieces of me
you can't have

aren't there
More Important Things
to worry about?
you ask

yes
there are

      Missing and Murdered Indigenous Relatives
          language revitalization
               extractive violence to lands and waters
             Native healthcare
                  incarceration
                  youth suicide
             heartbreak
          devastation
       tragedy
    ~~disparity~~ despairity

this list is never-ending
and everything on it is linked to the
art and symbols and ceremony and culture
you hijack for a quick, on-trend dollar

you act like you care about those
More Important Things
you don't
we get that
remember
we've been here before

but
you've been here before, too
#YesAllColonizers
have the privilege of
repeating their errors
  over and
    over and
      over
because you never stole land and
you never enslaved people and
that was so long ago, anyway and
you worked hard for that
trust-funded college education and
promotion to a job no one of color has ever held

and so what if you
live in a gentrified neighborhood and
eat the vegan diet for which
brown bodies and lands are exploited
the **Bad Thing** has never happened to you
so it's probably never happened at all
  over and
    over and
      over
privilege is a helluva drug, ennit

but
we see you
and unlike indian mascots and
halloween costumes and
dreamcatcher tattoos
we're authentic AF
coming at you with
600 years of receipts

we're relearning our languages
reclaiming our lands
protecting our waters
tearing down border walls
casting our ballots
saying NO!
to colonizer validation and
reminding you with every call out that
cancel culture and
political correctness
are just MAGA-speak
for accountability and respect

make no mistake
this is life and death for us
and we are not here for your entertainment

in fourteen hundred ninety-two
Columbus sailed for Asia true
but lost, got he, this Genoan chap
unsure East from West—who needs a map?

    upon thriving earth, Columbus' ships did land
    islands filled with many a child, woman, and man
    despite the Taino Arawak, people Columbus did
        proclaim
    "'Tis the Indies (or whatever)! I declare it for
        Spain!"

the wayward explorer could do no wrong
his wit was short as his sword was long
he demanded piles of gold from Tainos there
when he got some, then none, he did despair

    so he murdered and pillaged and raped with abandon
    all of which he journaled and recorded from his
        cabin
    and to the royals of Spain, he did report
    "To bodies, not gold, we shall resort."

for Columbus had found—yes, discover he did
a new use for the savages on whose mortal parts the
        wealthy bid
money for slaves, his voyages he could salvage
and salvage his name ('cause dehumanizing Natives
        grants modern day passage)

        instead of "navigationally challenged," he could
            be credited
        with discovering America (**history edited**)
        nevermind the millions already here
        most would be dead in a few hundred years

now this savvy enslaver, this terrorist bloke
leaves a legacy of deadly ignorance, making America the
        greatest joke
as the masses cry "Hero!" and celebrate discoverish
        deeds
Indigenous peoples continue to bleed

        assault, rape, human trafficking, and death
        Columbus squeezed 'til we breathed our last breath
        and today—his enduring bequest—our women still
            struggle for air
        we go missing and murdered, and… nobody cares

and our kids, oh, our kids! have lies shoved down their
        throats
their history books filled with fairytale boats
"Columbus Day" we recognize every October
fabrications and falsehoods repeated over and over

        and yet
        and YET
        the stage has been set
        by allies and relatives all covered in sweat

fighting to educate our lawmakers and kids
"fix school curriculums!" we demand, **"colonizer myths
     we forbid!"**
we march and we protest and we tear down his statues
"abolish Columbus Day! stop exalting his abuse!"

    and while ridding the world of this monstrous
        wrongdoing
    we find ourselves growing and evolving and pursuing
    new heights to our knowledge better ways to
        progress
    inclusion is possible with these grievances
        redressed

we ask all to consider—no, really, think bigger
so big a **BOOM!** sounds in your brain's pulled trigger
let's honor this land's first people, we say
join us in celebrating **Indigenous Peoples Day**

I'm only Native on federal holidays
between the hours of 1-3 p.m.
so stop calling about my rez ride's
extended warrantee

I snatch crystals and dreamcatcher tattoos
from Urban Outfitters employees
because goddammit
Custer died for this

I have a face more John Smith than Matoaka
but the fact that I know this name
gives me automatic brown points
like white bread getting that lightly toasted treatment

Twitter asks if I prefer Native American
or American Indian
that's when I whip out my Sierra Club-issued
certificate of authenticity
which incidentally is also my coffeehouse punch card
one more stamp to that mythic
tax-free life, baby

this is the first step toward reclamation
and the first line of my land acknowledgement

Happy Native American Heritage Month

I want a Lakota for President.

I want someone who can make something from nothing — like frybread or peace — for president.

I want someone who's been owned by a rez dog for president.

I want someone who makes a plate for their elders first for president.

I want plus-size auntie energy for president.

I want someone who's been held accountable by their tribe—and grandma—for president.

I want someone who knows #LandBack is praxis, not philosophy, for president.

I want someone humble enough to use spirit beads in their work for president.

I want someone who's smudgy, not judgy, for president.

I want someone who values both urban life and rez life for president.

I want someone willing to stand face-to-face with government agents in defense of their land and water relatives for president.

I want someone who lives Mitákuye Oyásiŋ for president.

I want a treaty defender for president.

I want someone who's spent time in an IHS waiting room for president.

I want someone who understands language is culture is language for president.

I want an unhyphenated Two Spirit for president.

I want someone who values community over bootstraps for president.

I want someone who doesn't feed any metaphorical wolves inside themselves for president.

I want someone who doesn't hang or tattoo dreamcatchers for president.

I want someone with a double-digit cousin count for president.

I want someone brave enough to reject blood quantum for president.

I want a merciless Indian savage for president.

I want a Lakota for President.

Inspired by Zoe Leonard.

41

Pre-heat oven to 1,492 degrees
Grease the pan with slavery and disease
In a large bowl mix land grabs with broken treaties
Stir in massacres, long walks, and boarding school ABCs

Don't forget the commodity cheese!

Set your table of white lies
With side dishes full of fairytale allies
Stuff your face with a main course of genocide
And wash it down with the tears of those still
    dehumanized

Indian mascots are the after-feast prize!
Ease your guilt with a warm slice of good intensions
While you cheer on harassment in activist mentions
Reflect gratitude for the stolen lands you occupy with
    sacred selfie pretensions
Cleanse your black (Friday) soul with a mass-produced
    sage kit ascension

Guaranteed good vibes for the low cost of cultural
    appropriation!

Praise the bountiful harvests of illegal resource
	extracting
Pick at the leftovers of Indigenous women colonial
	violence keeps subtracting
Settle in for pandemic anxiety due to visiting
	maskholes not masking
Fall asleep bursting with starch and privilege—purged
	of all Native issues distracting

Happy Thanksgiving!

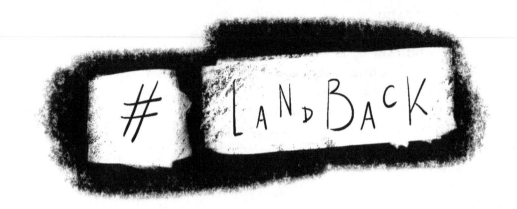

I've been trying to connect
with the land my whole life
but I've never had the language to do so

speaking with **the land is a puzzle**
colonialism scattered across generations

and it's likely my great-grandchildren
will still be picking up the pieces

so I pick up trash with my family
we spend weekends and holidays
amid public parks and open spaces
dismantling rubbish

we collect the fragments of humanity
cigarette butts, wrappers
and plastic — always plastic
we fill bags and bags
it never feels like enough

so we leave the best of ourselves
service and prayer — the same things, really
for the land

at home we pick up seeds
hold them like fragile wishes before sending
them back into the earth

plant medicine
introduced by elders, friends
and digital talking circles

sage and sweetgrass
cedar and tobacco
greasewood and prickly pear
and the three sisters
merging our bodies and spirits

I pick up their names with my heart
their syllables uttered like a prayer
practicing in Lakota and other Indigenous languages
others have the patience to teach me

pezíhota and wacáŋga
haŋté and caŋlí
ségai and nohwi
wagméza, omníca
and wagmú

my tongue scatters their sounds
clumsy with Western habits
they listen regardless

I've managed to pick up a few pieces of the puzzle
admiring the history of sparkling stones
thumbing the arboric Braille of bark
caressing secrets from leaves and petals
sharing blood thorned from pricked skin
dark soil sifting through fingers searching for stories

I thank the land for their gift of being
make it promises I hope to fulfill
we don't yet know the other's language, so I smile
and a week or a month later blooms smile back at me
I sing them ceremony songs and Broadway hits
to let them know who I am
we are relatives

I want the land back, yes
but even more
I want the land to want me back
each the other's missing piece
our jigsaw edges fitting together
in a long-awaited embrace

I am tired

my profile
twists in an unending battle cry
or stoic resignation
I yearn for peace

instead
I am held up for all to behold
dead
decapitated
like enemies of old
posted at the gates
or on jerseys
to frighten and to warn

a sacrifice
to the gods of entertainment
bashed
smashed
and tomahawk chopped
into co-opted cultural pieces so small
you don't even notice the stereotypes

from a bygone era I was displaced
created to celebrate the vanishing race
that's still right here!
conquered by disease
broken treaties
and state-sanctioned genocide
no, really, we're STILL HERE!

our stolen lands and stolen images annexed
by the Sports Industrial Complex
winner takes all

and we losers get **honor** forced down our throats
a spoonful of colonial cure-all
our kids and cultures and languages enthralled
held captive by the devotees of **good intentions**
and folks just fulfilling their occupations

ours are trophies of gaudy face paint
dyed chicken feathers
and drunk dude bros blethering on about a *fair* game

for more than a half-century
my people have begged for my freedom
and their own dignity
people can't be mascots, we say
you point to cowboys and padres and vikings
like you can align an entire continent
of sovereign nations
with **glorified job descriptions**

actual people can't be mascots, we say
and you tell us the Irish were enslaved
looks at the camera
and dust off a fabled Native ancestor
to justify your racism
the mental gymnastics needed to support these claims
is clearly the true sport here

I promise
the world won't end
when I transcend these demonic smiles
heal these violent scowls

let me close my eyes
retire the merchandise
turn the horses and drums and fake leather
out to pasture

delete the tribal font
the détente extends
with every buried axe and arrowhead
buy dinner for that one Native who said
I'm not offended by mascots
scrub the faux tan from your team's aught soul
take control of your own honor

let me rest

I.

i can't imagine
what life would be like today
  if our relationship with Treaty lands
  north of the north platte river
  and east of the big horn mountains
  had remained unbroken

  if we had been able to navigate the future
  and its many changes
  on our own terms

i want to conjure images of
lush landscapes and
healed hillsides
filled with flourishing relations amongst
  people
    beast
      plant
        place
          and time
but i am limited by my own colonized experiences
my what ifs spoiled with what is
a storyteller
  without a story to tell

II.

in a Treaty-honored world
maybe i'd create this poem in Lakota
    unhurried and
    unworried about spelling
and you'd be laughing because
instead of a tragedy
    i'd be telling a funny story to
    kids with land-toned skin
    about how colonizers thought they could
    own lands and people
ha! as if!
the wakáŋyeja would scoff
you can't own what is alive!
and we'd chuckle about all those silly settlers
    over meals we'd never worry would trigger diabetes

in a Treaty-honored world
maybe i'd write about how
    instead of pleading for
    adequate government funding
    for safety net programming
        while worrying about the
        latest Indigenous woman
        to go missing or found murdered
            after protesting yet another pipeline
            another mine
            or another illegal land grab
i would tell you about the ways
we cherish our Two Spirit medicine people
  we follow our bold and clever women leaders
    we learn from our wise and patient elders
      we trust our men as warriors and caregivers
        we love our happy and healthy children

in a Treaty-honored world
maybe we'd hold up
THE TREATY — all caps, baby
as a holy document
revered and remembered annually during
Treaty History Month
    as children across the world learn about
    mighty changemakers like
        Mapíya Lúta and
        Tatáŋka Íyotake and
        Ptesáŋwiŋ
    in school and
    at home and
    in blockbuster movies

in a Treaty-honored world
maybe i'd walk to and from the trading market
Fort Smith
    which everyone pronounces "smeet"
        because it's a really hard name to pronounce
    and so named to reclaim a space
        once used for intimidation and suppression
    and now used to support a
        thriving Indigenous economy
    and there i'd trade
    dark stories about what might have happened if
    THE TREATY
    hadn't been signed
people would shoo me away and say
    wóyake wiŋyaŋ, you must get your pessimism
    from your ancestor Chief Hump!
who didn't sign
THE TREATY
because he didn't trust the colonizers
and i'd say
    yeah, i know, but… what if?
and we'd all shake our heads at my mishegoss

in a Treaty-honored world
maybe we don't have to say things like
sacred land
     because to do so would imply that
     Océti Sakówiŋ territory
     wasn't already sacred
     because it just is
     and has always been

in a Treaty-honored world
maybe something like cultural appropriation
doesn't exist
     because it's inconceivable to have so little power
     that we need death grips around
          art and
              symbols and
                   adornments and
                       prayer and
                          ceremony
     because instead of being stolen from us
     we share these things
     with gratitude and humility
     because every day
     people see us modeling
     what it means to be good relatives
     to each other and the life around us

in a Treaty-honored world
maybe families aren't ripped apart by
     abuse
         addiction and
             youth suicide
because we're using ancestral knowledge
     of the medicines all around and within us
     in ways that reject exploitation and harm
and we embrace holistic justice and wellbeing

and we embrace communal
      self
            space and
                        time
so that no one
      especially our young people
feels abandoned

in a Treaty-honored world
perfection still doesn't exist and
      pain still rears its ugly head
and i know there's no guarantee that
      left to manifest our own destinies
      we wouldn't have also made terrible decisions
but... what if?

III.

today's settlers love to dissolve
our anti-colonial dreams
with shouts of
      cell phones!
      indoor plumbing! and
      denim jeans!
as if we didn't already have
      advanced communication systems
      excellent hygiene practices and
      clothing perfectly suited to our needs
as if those things were a good trade for genocide
they weren't

and i'd like to think
my people would have created
technologies in harmony with the world around them
      like

```
        i'm pretty sure solar-powered hover cars
        and gender-neutral clothing to flatter all sizes
        would already be a thing by now
if we had been left in charge


these what ifs
make my mind feel like a vast, unseeded prairie
        empty and struggling to imagine where
        the Océti Sakówin Confederacy
        would be today had
```

THE TREATY

```
        remained in accordance with its
        legally binding terms
                perhaps even serving as a standard for other
                Indigenous nations
```

instead
i am only able to imagine what
    i don't want
    in a Treaty-honored world
because everything i want in this world
    is tainted with a settler's gaze
        and a complete misunderstanding of
        community-based wellness
        and what it even looks like to thrive
colonization has left me as a sour fruit
    devoid of the ability to produce
    more than the barest taste of sweet

IV.

and yet
these what ifs
compel memory and witness
    of the once and future
    Océti Sakówiŋ Confederacy
in the time of
    THE TREATY
    and beyond
i want to tell you

about a nation so powerful
    the united states government was
    brought to its knees and
    forced to relinquish lands so rich with resources
        extractive pirates
        have barely scratched the
        surface of its potential
    nearly 150 years after the
    illegal discovery of gold

about a nation so clever and cunning
        it negotiated a land base
        roughly the size of spain
        away from enemies for a length of time
                no shorter or longer than
                forever

about a nation so superior
        its military might and skill led to the closure of
                not one
                        not two
                                but three
        key forts along the bozeman trail
        forts that Red Cloud and his warriors
                reclaimed with fire
                as u.s. soldiers abandoned them

about a nation so sovereign
        its people could choose their own lives to lead
                hunters
                        farmers
                                medicine people
        their children educated in dignified ways
        and its leaders deciding who entered and
                lived upon its Treaty lands

about a nation so at its zenith
        that the united states
                resorted to lies and deceit
                        broke their own rules and laws
                                massacred the weak and
                                        embarked on genocidal campaigns
        in an attempt to defeat us
        and still
                we never ceded our Treaty lands

V.

maybe writing about what could have been
        is the more entertaining story
but most of us never get the opportunity
        to learn more than the
        whitewashed version of events
        of what actually unfolded
we're told of disorganized and undisciplined savages
        who got lucky a few times
that Treaties
        were gifts to a vanishing race
        from a greater government
                a pen's stroke between mercy and massacre

TrEaty

wE haVe
YoUR
lANd

we're never told the story
      the truth
of the badassery that was
      is
the Océti Sakówiŋ Confederacy

no
it wasn't our nation being forced into a treaty
but the united states meeting our every demand
      acknowledging Océti Sakówiŋ superiority
our nation forced to play the colonizer's game
      and winning

can we turn what ifs into what nows
 can we reenergize and reorganize
  can we invoke critical remembrance
   can we demand thrivance over survivance
    can we unify and inform our present with our past
     can we create and nurture future relations

yes
and i can't wait to tell you
the story of how we did just that

Inspired by the 1868 Fort Laramie Treaty.

LAKOTA

OUROBOROS

Sioux, they called the Océti Sakówiŋ. An enemy snake.
Untrustworthy. Sneaky. A sssslur.
Serpents get a lot of bad press.
Tempting and unclean, snakes slither the Earth,
biblically bad and poisoning lands as slick, black,
oil-filled pipes.
Our paradise lost to the colonizers.

But we've no quarrel with snakes.
Like these relatives, we are cunning and patient.
The Océti Sakówiŋ don't even need hands to fuck you up.
We hiss not to warn, but to promise.
Stepping on us is a big mistake.
Leave us alone.

The Océti Sakówiŋ are people of water and fire.
Complimentary elements our existence depends upon.
There's power in being a snake.

Our bodies undulate with dancing flames
and rushing streams.
We twist and coil, ever in motion.
Sometimes a ripple, sometimes a surge.

Like Water. Like Fire.
Océti Sakówiŋ bodies are flooded with story.
One that's burned into our DNA tells of a Great Race
amongst animal and human relatives.
A marathon like no other that continues today,
ever-moving and constant, circling Pahá Sápa.

We are a snake chasing its own tail.
Creation out of destruction. Life out of death.
We endure. We are the Océti Sakówiŋ.

Call us *Sioux*, if you're ignorant.
Like a snake, our identity bows and flexes,
curls in on itself to slough off the bad,
allowing the shiny armor underneath to glisten.

On our backs we carry the next seven generations.
The Océti Sakówiŋ set ourselves ablaze
so others may rise from our ashes.
The smoke from our charred bones
snakes through the air to carry our prayers
in a ceremonial dance toward the clouds.
And the Great Race carries on through oceans of blood
memory infused with our unflinching, bottomless love.

Flowing. Balanced. Our scales forever tipped
in a repeating pattern for the future.
So go ahead and call us snakes.
The Océti Sakówiŋ are never-ending.

✝ ✝ ✝ ✝

TOO SPIRIT

there are scars on my body
where i imagine you might have touched me
fairytales on my upper arms and inner thighs
mythologies grazing an ankle and teasing my wrists
but i closed those books
just before the climax

too ashamed of these spirited feelings for you
i released them in a ritual bloodletting
night after night
slicing my spirit into jagged halves
fighting over whether my story would end
with a period or a semicolon
each cut a confession of every kiss
i wanted us to share

good catholic girls don't want to kiss
good catholic girls
not in north dakota

so i sacrificed pieces of my flesh
for an impossible fantasy
too spirited to exist
at 17 i tried to *come out*
i didn't yet have words like bisexual
or gender nonconforming

so i said i was gay
the same way i might tell someone
the science of black holes
with a shrug
a shake of my head
and an apology for daring
to think i could ever explain
something of which i had
so little knowledge
and possessed too much

my gayness was like a black hole
it sucked
all-consuming
there was nothing left for others to do
except pray the gay away
and me right along with it
so i closed this book, too
and went *back in*

it took several years
a few states
lots of college
and even more therapy
to understand how too much spirit
and black holes
complement each other
complement me

my spirit had never been *too* anything
but *two*
as in more than the sum of any one explanation
more than any one's expectation
not a black hole to disappear
but a portal to untold ancestral knowledge

i searched for the pieces of myself i had cut away
clumsily gluing them back together with Lakota stories
of people exalted for what we call queerness
before untranslatable words and heart medicine
were destroyed in the fires of colonial patriarchy
these stories describe roles and responsibilities
for people who embody transcendent spirits
and it was these stories that called me back to myself

I have mourned the words that tried to come out with me
and I have mourned words turned to ash
I'm 37 now - it's two decades, countless ceremony
and all.the.therapy later
I am well into my role as a Wóoyake Wíŋyaŋ
and learning the medicines of Wiŋyaŋ Witkó
I am creating my own words for what has always been
always been here and there and within

words that look and feel
like something beyond gender or religion or politics
something like accountability and purpose
the scars I carry tell the stories of my love
for you, yes, but more for myself, the ancestors,
and the next seven generations
for the land and language I'm reconnecting with

they itch with eagerness
rooting for me to level up, decolonize-style
so I have repurposed these scars into constellations
stories across the universe of my body
a map I can follow
back to the most sacred parts of myself
and reminding me of everything that has fought
for this Two Spirit to exist

+ + + +

VIOLENCE IS A TIME MACHINE

someTimes
I can't sleep
forget the last few miles
of the morning commute
zone out in a meeting
or at the dinner table
it's the idle fingers of my brain
picking at the never-healed wounds of my worst moments

the urge to scratch at no-good memories
gets triggered by anything, anywhere
a scent or a flash of color hijacks my present
transporting me back to the exact moment
my future diverged from normalcy
trapped by hands still holding me down
after all these years

someone — somemany
trespassed against my body
violated my mind
offering no serenity, only eternity
reaching through Time to steal from me

they took then and they take now
even if they no longer draw breath
mine comes up short
heart racing, palms sweaty
something else goes missing
things as a 3-year-old
I didn't even know I would need or want one day
things decades of therapy and small pills
are still trying to help me recover

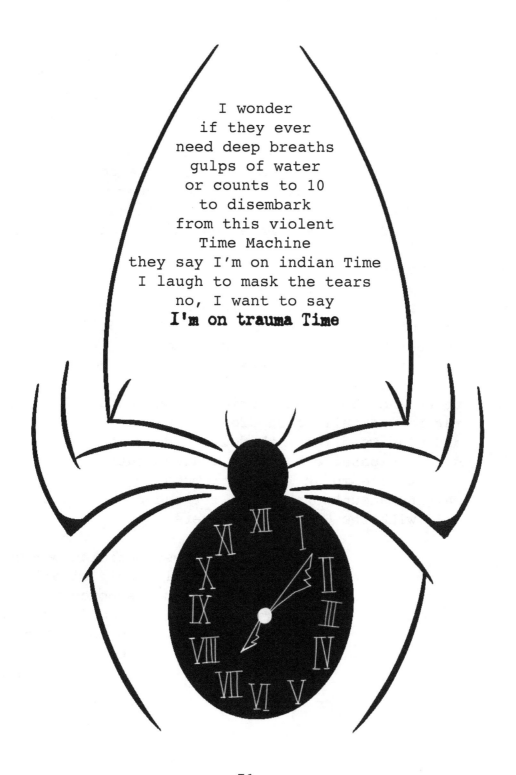

I wonder
if they ever
need deep breaths
gulps of water
or counts to 10
to disembark
from this violent
Time Machine
they say I'm on indian Time
I laugh to mask the tears
no, I want to say
I'm on trauma Time

                         fragile like a bomb
                       my counterfeit body
                       this hotchkiss heart
                      these canary lungs
                    anxiously ticking down to
                                     nothing
                     because I explode on repeat
        and now it's too late to file a police report
                  or make it out to dinner with friends
                           it's all the same thing
           Time is violence rewinding itself unkindly

I seek Timelessness
those everyday magic tricks
that transform little things into big things
        embraces that outlast my attempts to pull away
        gut-busting wordplay and charades
        exploring prairies, lakes, mountains, deserts,
              oceans, and Netflix
        texts and phone calls bridging thousands of miles
        fur babies full of cuddles
        and windows filled with flourishing green things
        gender expansive butterfly transformations
              to steampunk warrior femmes
        walking an unknown but well-tread parenting path
              with the Ojibwe Mr. Rogers

                              these medicine moments
                offer profound comfort in their simplicity
                   it's here Time shares its power with me
                                        abracadrabra
                                    and for a second
                                    or an eternity
                                    I am at peace

Learn the secrets of fire
My child
And set your soul aflame

Incinerate the spreading underbrush
        of toxic expectations
Rid your forests and plains of the invasive
        politics of being

Let your blaze clear a path for sunshine
Thrive in the ashes
And let the knowledge of dead things nourish your roots

Understand you are in control of the spark
        in your heart
Know it is fueled by the ancestral love
        ever surrounding you

Whenever the tumbleweeds of settler guilt
        overrun your path
Or a thicket of colonizer trash
        precludes you from reaching your dreams
Rekindle the fires

Let the flares dance
        to the rhythm of your laughter
And be a signal to relatives everywhere
The cleansing inferno begins again

Ilé: Lakota word meaning "to be burning."

THE
Sovereignty
OF
Humor

There's an expression
with many uses and
many meanings.
It's more than a word.
More than a sound.
In every utterance
it evokes fun.
Ayeeee

It's a jab. A punchline.
A joke unto itself.
It's verbal currency.
Better than a passport.
A priceless family heirloom.
The maker of relatives.
Ayeeee

In grade school we learned about
American Indians
or at least the stoic
Edward Curtis version
of how Indians were supposed to look.

The "vanishing" race —
a people sad and depressed and all but extinct.
We could be vicious, too
in movies and history books.
But always we were defeated.
And no one wants to be
on the losing side.
These images
these stereotypes
of an ever-frowning people
contrast sharply with the
laughter and jokes
of the tióspaye I grew up with.

Sure, there are low moments —
like, down-to-the-last-dollar and
oh-my-god-call-the-police low —
but in all that we find reasons to smile
reasons to cheese out, commod-style.

And that's the thing about Native humor.
It's kept us alive.
Ayeeee
— and all it represents —
isn't just for entertainment.
It's an endurance tactic.
   Like
      air
         water
            food
               and shelter
our people need humor to thrive.

Ayeeee
recognizes what we have survived together.
It's a sorry-not-sorry testament to shouldering
the crushing weight of
   poverty
      genocide
         diabetes
            boarding schools
               massacres
                  addiction
                    and Disney's Pocahontas.

Without the protective armor of Ndn humor
we'd be dead inside.
Ndn humor says
NOT TODAY COLONIZER.
Ayeeee

Ndn humor reclaims the life
hate and fear and Manifest Destiny
have tried to remove and assimilate.
    Resistance is only futile
    if you can't laugh about it later
    because you realize a belly-jiggling guffaw
    pulls you up better than any
    philosophical bootstrap.

Ndn humor recognizes the irony
in celebrating code talkers who saved WWII
with the same languages
their country tried to beat out of them as kids
    and the irony in denying voting rights
    to the people who had lands stolen
    and treaties broken
    to form a democracy modeled after the Constitution
    of the Haudenosaunee Confederacy.

Ndn humor mocks those who say
racist mascots are an honor
as they whoop and chant like the
tomahawk-wielding savage their ancestors killed.

Ndn humor mocks the stupidity of
white Hollywood saviors
like Kevin Costner's wolf-waltzing John Dunbar
and Johnny Depp's taxidermically adorned Tonto.

Ndn humor mocks every claim to Cherokee royalty
that conveniently ignores Cherokee struggle.
Ndn humor mocks the ridiculous disrespect
of hipster headdresses:
Yes, those hot pink chicken feathers sure are sacrit.
Get over it, you say.
Trust us - we're *so* over your bullshit.
It's *you* that can't seem to let go of *our* identity.

Ndn humor winks at the camera
when Native women overtake
the same government systems
that refuse to protect them
from going missing and murdered
    and winks again when the same face masks
    police ripped off protectors at Standing Rock
    must now be worn to save lives from a virus
    fueled by climate change.

Ndn humor is dark hair thick with greasy secrets
you wish you knew
and cheekbones that can cut down bad spirits.
Ayeeee!

    It's your grandma's squinty, tear-filled eyes
    and soft, wrinkled hand
    covering her toothless grin.
        It's your sister's head thrown back
        a gut-busting cackle
        spewing from her defiant smile
        as she slaps your arm — hard.
            Ndn humor is your uncle
            teasing you relentlessly
            with love-filled lessons
            And you eventually learn
            the joke is your ego
            So be humble, dammit.

Ndn humor reminds anyone who forgets we are still here.
It builds up the next generations and tells them at
every opportunity not to turn back but to keep going
into the future.

Ndn humor is a sovereign act
and our laughter is medicine.
It is the battle cry of aunties everywhere:
Ayeeee!

+ + + +

I want you
an ache
deep in my core drives me
to collect the pieces of you
scattered around
like raw promises
waiting for me to feast

I lick my lips
salivating at the thought
of your splintered fragments
coming together and reforming
into something beyond both of us
it makes me **come** undone
I work my fingers through a mound
of your sticky recipe
kneading every part of you
letting you rise
just   high   enough

you like it rough
a slap here   a pull there
tugging   pressing   stoking the fire
and stretching your limits
until gently   so gently
I lay you flat
not to rest   but to burn

you writhe for me
sizzling with expectation
I wait   impatient
and hungry for you
it is ecstasy to watch your hills and valleys
slick and glistening and drowning in the pop song
of anointed blue birds

but we're not finished

just as you're about to **combust**
I flip you and start the mad process over
your body undulates for me
and suddenly   you're hot   brown perfection
is ready   and so is my tongue

sometimes we play around
with honey when you're feeling
soft   sweet   and warm
or sometimes we get wild   like rice
but tonight   there's only meat
lettuce experiment on your commod bod
with dairy-free cheese
that melts in my mouth   and my hand

round in all the right places
your lovely lumps taste so good
and **I moan your name**
thanking the ancestors for the gift
that will forever sit upon my soul   and thighs
you are my deliciously undeniable **Frybread**

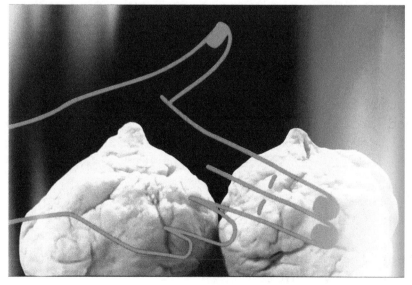

Artwork by Taté Walker

THE STRONG FRIEND

you say I need to learn
how to take a compliment
that I resist them
like stormtrooper blaster fire

"Your work ethic is amazing!" *dodge*
"You're so organized!" *twist*

"Nothing rattles you. You're so held together." *duck*
"I wish I were as independent as you." *block*

"You're so strong/brave/confident!"
jump in the trash chute

I say thank you
and it comes out like an apology
you call me humble
but I'm just waiting for you to leave me forever

every compliment feels like a proton torpedo that
if aimed precisely enough
could trigger a total system collapse
of my carefully constructed "I'm fine!" façade

what I mean is: I'm still learning how not to be bitter
about the things you find most appealing about me
like
my attention to the details no one cares about
and burn-out hyperdrive

84

pair nicely with the anxious perfectionism
of never being good enough
or
this insistence I can do it Solo
while cracking a joke conceals emotions
I've locked away so they can never again
be trampled by someone I trust

what I mean is: your strong friend is not OK
I hold the Dark Side at bay by cleaning all the things

existing within never-ending survival mode
makes me second-guess everything
my headspace is a C-3PO mess worried
about the things I can't change

so I Force-choke my heartspace
and force a smile on my face
because it feels easier
to let you think I've got it all under control
but
I'm dismantling these trauma-built barriers
and learning to ask for help
which sometimes looks like
an ignored text
canceled dates
and pop-culture humor

what I mean is: my love language
is persistent care, not praise
And **you love me**
I know

✦ ✦ ✦ ✦

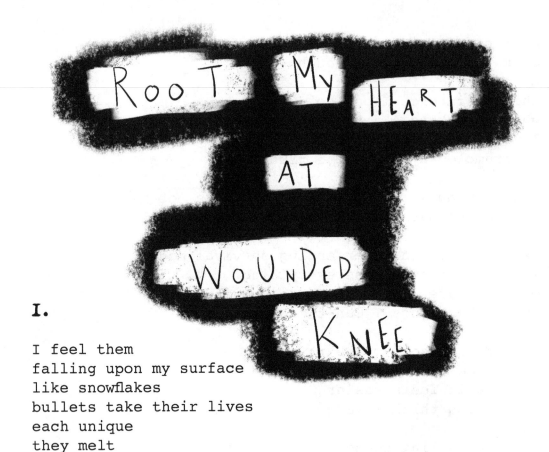

ROOT MY HEART AT WOUNDED KNEE

I.

I feel them
falling upon my surface
like snowflakes
bullets take their lives
each unique
they melt
and their hearts return to me
Wounded Knee

I try to be a soft place to land
but the land is closed
for the season of white
colonizing my every curve and crevice
their menace leaves me
bruised
abused
scarred
I am a deathbed for these hearts
I hold like fruit forced too soon from the tree
atop
Wounded Knee

I measure this time as a singer at a drum
wailing to the sound of so many thumps
no rhythm
just the echo of broken promises on ice
a dream heist
set to a savage soundtrack
with a Hotchkiss base beat
and they sing

> *give up your land, and we won't kill you*
> *live on this reservation, and we won't kill you*
> *stop dancing, stop singing, and we won't kill you*
> *we won't kill you*
> *we won't kill you*

a viciously victorious dirge they dedicate
to my Relatives who flee
Wounded Knee

such entreaties make it easy
for wasícu — *the fat takers*
to see lives like lands
and resource extraction becomes target practice on
the bodies of those who only want to protect me
survival is the priority
you throw your hands up
wave a white flag
and hope
surrender doesn't make you
an easier mark
now the Oceti Sakowin are
slowly dying of survival
the denial of life
stains the frozen ground
like a smear of war paint
across the bloody
Wounded Knee

II.

sometime later
my frozen arms are pried open
inch by inch
six feet
300 bodies
the stink of
destinies
and doctrines
and discoveries
and fear
fuels the digging
a grave seems to be the only place
Indigenous people are allowed to gather
en masse
interred
    in massacre
the wasícu give their promises
back to the Lakota
and bodies back to me
Wounded Knee

I accept this forced sacrifice
as a gift
the Pté Oyáte are returning home
not alone
but accompanied by
scars and wounds
each a prayer   ·
on skin the same shades
of my warm hills and prairies
marked skin that tells me
they lived lives worth fighting for
and my brother
the Creator
will know them all as worthy of rest
they fill me with death
and in death
life
I turn to their waiting spirits above
and say through the crisp, winter air

   rejoice, Relatives
   for your bodies are welcome below
   return your spirits to the stars
   and watch this ultimate offering
   fertilize the next seven generations

their hearts sink into me
not buried, but
composted
soiled beauty
under
Wounded Knee

III.

my earth blankets these bodies
I smile to myself
as I tuck them in
the enemy doesn't understand
can't understand
that they sow the seeds
of resistance
a persistent force
that will never remain buried
for I know the slow, steady ways of the root
an unceasing underground ceremony
a spreading memory planted anew
blooming resistance
counting coup
and screaming into the face
of white supremacy

**MY DREAM IS OLDER THAN AMERICA
AND WILL BE HERE LONG AFTER**

so I will hold these hearts
like I hold all sacred seeds
and watch their roots grow
to one day grasp hold of all that's been settled
returning the invasive burdens
like all decaying things
to me
Wounded Knee

I.

our tale begins
with a well-mannered Lakota woman
Tapúŋ Sá Wiŋ

this beauty marries a   star man
goes to live with his people in the cloud
gets pregnant
succumbs to loneliness
tries to climb down to her people
fails   and falls to her death

the baby survives
grows up to accomplish all the things
and returns to the sky world
to watch over his relatives below

the end

II.

this black hole of a story
sucks away   everything
from Tapúŋ Sá Wiŋ
Red Cheek Woman

and still has the audacity to use her name
as if eternal glory is a men-only club
her value rests solely in what
draws the male gaze
    her beauty
    her ~~good manners~~ subservience
    and aforementioned red cheeks

she marries an attractive stranger
only to find out he lives in the freaking sky
away from everyone she knows and loves
with his judgmental grannie
the moral of this tale?
mighty fine homeboys come attached to some
mighty fine print
sure   you'll be on cloud nine for a while
until suddenly you're plummeting to Earth
like a dead star

knowing what *I* know about
Lakota women
I offer the following retelling

III.
there once was a free spirit
who paid little attention to
what others thought about her

her skin always held a   flushed hue
because she was constantly
in motion
    heart beating
    lungs laughing
    eyes shining
she painted small circles of red
across the apples of her cheeks

because she liked how the color
brought out her fierceness and confidence
like everyday   war paint
her physical beauty was striking
but paled in comparison to her
    strength
    vitality
    and compassion
which drew others to her
as moths to a flame
they couldn't touch but basked in her warmth

not one of these people would have accused
Tapúŋ Sá Wiŋ
of being   *well-mannered*
    respectful
    appreciative
    considerate
but not   *well-mannered*
putting   *well-mannered*
in the same sentence as *Lakota wiŋyaŋ*
let alone the same sentence as Tapúŋ Sá Wiŋ
is oxymoronic
    because only a moron
    would accuse a *Lakota wiŋyaŋ*
    or Tapúŋ Sá Wiŋ
    of being   *well-mannered*
it is known

for all this she called   herself
Tapúŋ Sá Wiŋ
Red Cheek Woman
    she liked to tease others by saying
    "you should see my other cheeks"
    while waggling her eyebrows and reading
    "Fifty Shades of Ayeeeee"
in this way she made the cheeks of others turn red

and that's why the people called   her
Tapúŋ Sá Wiŋ

when she felt ready to start a family
Tapúŋ Sá Wiŋ gathered the men and women
she was attracted to and said
"listen up fives, a ten is talking"
and proceeded to lay the ground rules for her courtship
     above all, you had to respect her
     and her love for her relatives
     because nothing was more important
     than family   except maybe eating tubers
it soon became clear the admirers
struggled to meet her high standards
and she dismissed them all   save one
     a smart, humble man who listened
     when Tapúŋ Sá Wiŋ spoke
        and especially when she didn't
     they had known each other their entire lives
     and Tapúŋ Sá Wiŋ knew him to be an
     honorable man as committed to his people
        as the North Star was to the night sky
"**tecihíla hca**" he told her on their seventh date
     I love you
"**he slolwáye**" she responded
     I know

and while the entire village celebrated the new couple
the more important part of this tale is that
Tapúŋ Sá Wiŋ was happy
     so happy the energy of her heart
     was like an explosion felt across the universe

IV.

lots of people will criticize this remake
    "it's *just* an old story"
    "leave it *alone*"
or
    "don't you know it's *really* about constellations?"
and
    "things were different *back then*"
    "Tapúŋ Sá Wiŋ still got to *choose* her husband"
    "look how *progressive* our society was"
then
    "what *other* cheeks?"
and
    "*what do you mean* Tapúŋ Sá Wiŋ
    was attracted to women?"

here's the thing
I'm just as grateful as the next Lakota
to have access to this traditional story
written and translated
about Tapúŋ Sá Wiŋ's son
and how much he valued
kinship

and not really about
the epic tragedy
that was
Tapúŋ Sá Wiŋ's
unexplored life

but tales like these
were never meant
to be canonized

Lakota storytellers
added context
and meaning

where it fit
    time
    circumstance
    and audience
changed
though many details stayed the same

oral history
isn't supposed to be
stagnant or dogmatic
as with life   stories are multifaceted and complex
galaxies of information waiting to be told and retold
like the cosmos dancing above earth
stories are meant to   evolve
    and progress
because that's what cultures do
    if we want to survive
and Indigenous women
    need to see themselves   thriving
    in the stories we tell

this rewrite isn't about
    feminism run amok
    or critiquing tradition
    or missing and murdered Indigenous women
    or pretending I know anything about storytelling
this is me   an unmannerly Lakota wiŋyaŋ
telling a simple story for Tapúŋ Sá Wiŋ

I'd like to imagine sharing this tale with her
that her dark eyes would have glittered with humor
    and joy
    a thousand everlasting suns blazing
    through space and time
her cheeks red from so much smiling

THE DARKEST EVERYTHING

i am buried so deep and dark
in your glorious universe
this obsidian space rich with unexplored life

> my joy stretches like
> summertime shadows
> felt in your vivid blacks and browns

shades of warmth and strength
protection against the bright white
that exposes all our faults and fears

> there's a lie in light
> burning us away from one another
> turning our underground ceremony to ash

tricking us into believing that dirt
with its endless possibilities for growth
is unclean

> glares try to colonize
> our hopes with dread and disdain for
> what the dark offers

as if the expansive unknown
isn't always a mysteriously murky adventure
where we find ourselves

> rooted and ready to bloom
> two spirits rising together with winter's new moon
> into the darkest everything

Inspired by Frida Kahlo.

+ + + +

I.
once upon a time the Earth was overrun
with those who filtered Themselves against reality
hiding behind perfection
and capitalism's illusions of security

They grammed and primed
while the world burned around Them
everything's fine, They tweeted alongside a photo of an
     "I Voted" sticker
baby steps and bootstraps, They reminded the rioters
just use a metal straw
and remember: not all white people
lol #like4like #makethisgoviral

when the Pandemic came
not even Google could save Them
They mixed boredom and privilege
into an infectious cocktail of meme-ific sinophobia
Am I worthy? They asked with every mundane rendition of
     the latest 20-second song

Their posts pleaded for connection
so They connected in the toilet paper aisle
spreading panic faster than any plague
quarantined, Their own company proved unbearable
even from behind 10,000-square-feet of living space

have hope, They said
as They tried to save the world
with Netflix and food delivery
wearing jammies in Their suburban and gentrified prisons

II.

there were Others, too, impacted by the Pandemic
but since they'd been practicing for — or forced into
lifelong social distancing

the bougie-panic seemed out of touch with the Others'
reality
> *wash our hands?*
> *some of us don't even have running water*
> > *the airlines might shut down?*
> > *and I was really looking forward*
> > *to that Fiji trip*
> > *once my ungodly student loan bill was paid off*
> > > *the sickness restricts breathing?*
> > > *it's killing folks?*
> > > *what — police, oil companies,*
> > > *and Republican health care policies*
> > > *are taking a break?*

the Others weren't being glib
the Others cared — the Others knew better than anyone
the disposability of life
for those considered "at-risk"
with or without the Pandemic

this latest epidemic represented
just another uncontrollable agent of Death
waiting to meet the Others
for a chance encounter on the subway,
    or on a sidewalk,
        or in a grocery store

the Others still had all the "ism"s and "phobia"s
pressing down upon them
what was a 20-second song really gonna do, anyway

III.
the Earth changed, as its wont to do
things that once seemed untouchable
    professional sports
        school calendars
            Tax Day
                police
                    prisons
                        capitalism
suddenly had their arbitrary natures exposed
pushing everyone to adapt and innovate
or be rendered obsolete

and those who had been Othered their entire existence
found themselves capable of weathering
panic-induced storms of empty shelves and isolation

the Others took charge and detonated long-buried
but oft-maintained
weapons of mass creation
mutual aid-based survival was in their genetic code
or at least in their coping strategies

the Ancestors of the Others had experienced
the plural of apocalypse
yes, the Others knew the destructive power
of a well-aimed germ
but also knew the ceremony secrets
of washing away toxins
knew community power could bridge any divide
knew medicine isn't only what a doctor prescribes
    but also what grows from the ground
        or from a laugh
            or from a social distance powwow

IV.

the Earth that bloomed from the Pandemic wasteland
flourished through love and selflessness

They thought the Pandemic would break the Others
but collaborative ceremonial art became the key
to open the door to the Other side
of this latest Armageddon

eventually, lost lands and languages were reclaimed
non-human relatives were returned
to their rightful place of honor
and the colonial endeavors that once extracted

the essence of humanity with every dollar earned
were dismantled

small communities of care emerged
from the mega-industries
and those with feminine energies
gifted the world with leadership
that transcended privilege and inequity

wellbeing spread like a virus
caught and held up like the sun
encircling the Earth with a corona of possibility

I.

That's weird.
Say it one more time.
Oh, I thought you said Katie.
Is it short for Tatiana?
Tater tot! Ha!
Rhymes with latte.

But like you're really Johnny, right?
Toddie. Todd-day. Taaaah tay. Tah TAY.
There's an accent? There's an e?
So, it's actually Tate.
Ugh. Whatever. It sounds made up.
You're so extra.
It's hard to type. Is Tate so bad?
Tate isn't technically a misspelling.
José and Chloë are actual names, though.

Get over it.

II.

this goes out to all the folx
with names too thick and too sticky
for colonized tongues to dominate
to those with names
rejected by baby books and gas station key chains
and whose name is always spelled wrong
on the invitation

this goes out to the folx
with names that fill uninitiated mouths
full of too many inconvenient syllables
so you learn to answer to extended "Heeeeys"
to those with names no one ever confuses with the
Sarahs and Shawns with an H
an H that never makes teachers stumble
to those who experience roll-call anxiety
and get strangled
with nicknames from playground bullies

this goes out to the folx
with delicacy names like choking hazards
so they cut you down to bite-size
mix you with raisins and mayonnaise
and drop pieces of you like crumbs
to find their way back to mediocrity
to those with names
translated into something more palatable
for people who think ketchup is spicy
but can pronounce Saoirse, Joaquin, and Charlize
with perfect emphasized love

this goes out to the folx
with names that get fumbled and dropped in the mud
only to be carelessly swept under a basic rug
and whitewashed into a sobriquet
or judged too difficult and sent to the DO NOT HIRE bin
to those with names too exotic for ignorant ears
too lazy to interrupt their status quo convos
to those with names accented with a symphony of notes
out of range to the tone-oblivious
so you get remixed with dead air
in concert halls of generic white noise

III.
remember
your sticky thickness tastes like honey
to the ones who named you
your mysteries admired and adored without translation

remember
no trendy trinket will ever hold up
to the timelessness of the alphabet
your ancestors recognize

remember
to enjoy the awkward blunders of the person
across from you suddenly forced to pay more attention
to a name that has survived eons of
    oceans
        explorers
            walls
                wars
                    conquistadors
                        settlers
                            genocide
                                the gender binary
                                    and public schools

make them carry the weight of your name
on a tongue that's done little
to no heavy lifting
ours are names that stretch the imagination
and lay the foundation to understanding
who we are and where we belong
we are not Shakespearian roses
to be called just anything
anyone lacking the perseverance to pronounce
and spell with humble accuracy
expose themselves as undeserving
of your truest magic

our names demand accountability
deserve practice
and exude prayer
our names are fields of immemorial beauty
seeded with story and song
ours are the names of ceremony
between the lips and the breath that created them
and especially if we created them ourselves

your delicious honey name
reminds the mouth how sweet
decolonized lips taste
when animated by totemic fluency
a dancing name full of vitality and memory
its worth noted in every digraph and glottal stop
a trove of diacritical treasures
only the worthy can find

TATÉ EMÁCIYAPI

IV.

They call me Taté.
The Lakota messenger god of Wind,
commanding the four directions.
Mother. Partner. A good relative.
Mine is a hard-earned title sparkling
with Two Spirit responsibility.
Mine honors my Mniconjou Lakota tióspaye.
A nod to the stardust in my veins.
A shout-out to the Milky Way ancestors.

Taté is a braid
tightened with the lyrical roundness of
Great Plains dynastic vowels
and the sacred medicine
of the prairie's punctuated consonants.

My name is Taté. There's an accent on the e.

slowly I unravel
the razzle dazzle
of my once tight lines maligned
by the weight
of your nightmares — kept awake
within fringed, plastic dreamcatchers
appropriators are culture-wearing body snatchers
I hang limp and dusty over your bed
a tradition left for dead

frantic I spiral
your crocodile smile
flashes sharp and jagged, a haphazard
slash at the many anchors I so carefully placed
onto your promises now tasting
empty and pulling at me
like a windswept broken treaty
my perfectly balanced world doomed
by your need to consume

my hard-spun universe gently crashes
floating ashes blasted
into the void
destroying ancestral history
like all indigenous mysteries
you blame aliens, try to erase my existence
only to discover I am resistant
a persistent tricksy spider
with silk and stories to spare

I am seven generations and five worlds worth of lives
striving and thriving
ready to leap off my back and attack
genocide and oppression
fangs out and dripping with justified aggression
swarming settler tables set for good-intentioned war
now feasts for us coloniavores
but no rest once we've eaten
radical responsibility hold accountable freedom

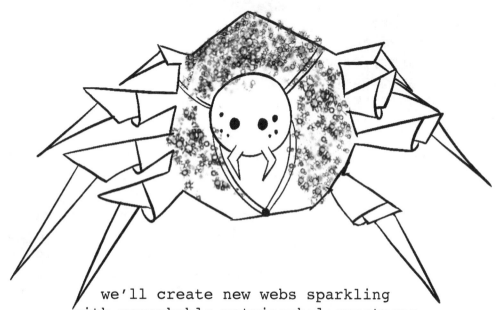

we'll create new webs sparkling
with remarkable matriarchal greatness
as weightless as a good dream just passing through
vowing to return, inspiring you
to pursue resilient love woven with Indigenous ideals
strung with tensile strength
5x that of extracted steals
the kinship patterns of our cosmic wheels
interconnect and hold those hearts ready to heal

tricksters are
unadulterated appetite
striking first, often directionless
instinct guiding these mythic wights
fueled by electric will
charged with Earth's delights
stoked by memory's flames
and in their wake jagged pathways
leading one from ignorance to erudite

no moral good nor immoral bad
just the reactionary Nature
of being here and now
the trickster heals our fractured Culture
with medicinal story
urging us to butcher
norms and status quo
a slyly effective relational tincture

Iktómi the Spider
played many roles in Lakota history
a proud icon
of Great Plains glory
a cunning weaver
of trickery
shapeshifting wicked webs
protective and predatory

Iktómi braids complex truths
from the pulsing toothache of sticky lies
we've happily choked down whole
gluttonous and oblivious to the demise
we precipitated through our collective inattention
Iktómi pulls a thread, forcing us to catch wise
Iktómi stalks our fears, snags our nightmares
Iktómi savors our tears, swallows our cries

this discomfort is necessary trickster tonic
the price of healing a world allergic to change
tricksters rip away both band aid and bride veil
exposing ranthoneous tongues and stagnant veins
to reality's spicy, pantomathic sting
when honesty clenches your throat with rage
when your raincloud eyes destroy all the dams
know that Iktómi uses lit dynamite to smudge sage

the four directions fill with smoke
as thick and obscure as Iktómi's intentions
the spider seeks the comfort of solitude's darkness
but lures visitors in
with sparkling geometric perfection
in this we learn that boundaries can both
build and obliterate community
Iktómi's murky motivations defy comprehension

I am Iktómi
a version created to disrupt
my body erupting with story
questioning social constructs
catapulting neon lies into the sandcastles
where status quo lives uninterrupted
my propane tales fill each room
a matchstick away from exposing settler corruption

115

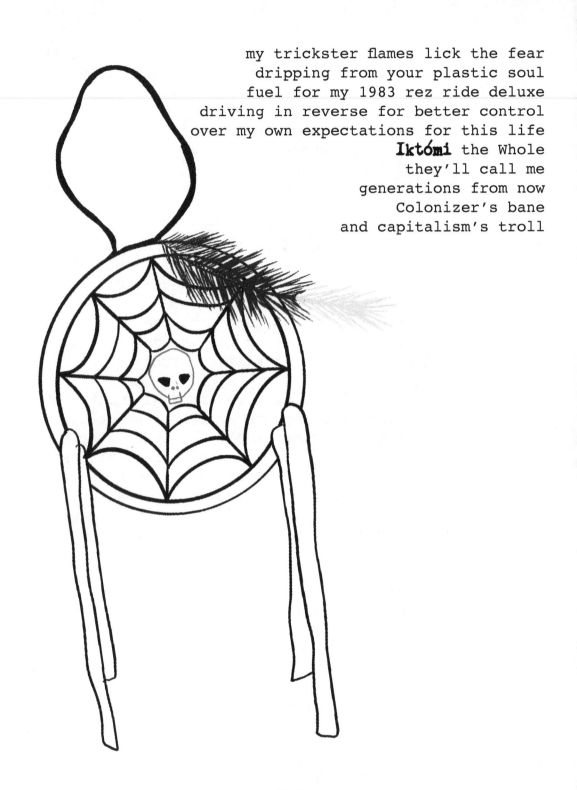

my trickster flames lick the fear
dripping from your plastic soul
fuel for my 1983 rez ride deluxe
driving in reverse for better control
over my own expectations for this life
Iktómi the Whole
they'll call me
generations from now
Colonizer's bane
and capitalism's troll

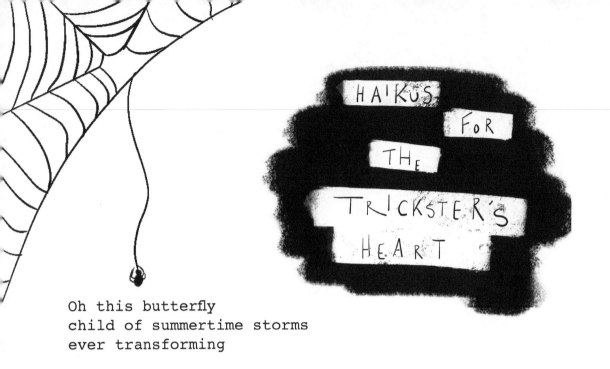

HAIKUS FOR THE TRICKSTER'S HEART

Oh this butterfly
child of summertime storms
ever transforming

My love language is
chores done. Food cooked. Loyalty
unconditional.

You can also find
Indigenous beads and bling
paving my heartpath.

lakeshores and empty
apartments hold the remnants
of whisper promises

in separate beds
love everlasts my absence
and your desire

cars are concert halls
for libras and lions, not
hermit fisherman

she shoulders immense
futures with fierce gentleness,
my older sister.

little brother could
ask me for anything and
I'd hand him the world

second chances from
little sister are worth all
the starry wishes

my mom made every
graduation even if
there was no invite

staring at the end
an empty heart in bare fields
I call for momma

our genetic joy
plants humor where once pain grew
love flourishes here

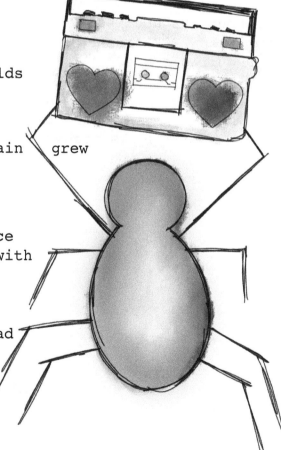

eyes bright sky blue pierce
through memory, drown me with
sandcastle passion

eating sandwiches
at a playground with my dad
he says it's our place

getting past the past
feels insurmountable sans
your apologies

resting in the back
the beagle waits for me to
play with her in the dirt

Stubbed tails and smol legs
can't mask the fierce fire of
two floofy feline queens

deep breaths of soil
breezes sigh promises in
my petrichor dreams

without the aunties
those few BFF crushes
I hemorrhage fire

this scaly sun this
horny moon rising crabby
seeks archers and goats

let's braid our grays as
one endless bond maské we
future ancestors

I read a meme once
that said sunflowers
will seek out
the brightest thing
and if they can't find the sun
they will turn
and face another sunflower
and I think maybe that's
what **true love** looks like

when I was four **true love** looked like
my parents wrapped in each other's drama
a divorce that eclipsed my childhood
within a decade-long custody battle
that taught me to be a skilled Libra
full of truths and lies
my face a pair of scales
struggling to balance the light of both parents
my mother the east and my father the west
moving farther and farther away from me

when I was 16 **true love** looked like my best friend
this kind of love gets you prayed away in North Dakota
so I hid that love in a dark closet
where my sunshine petals slowly fell away
she loves me not
adults pruned my leaves
mistaking blood for rot
and in bold desperation I plucked the brightest
bloom left of myself
I think I'm gay I said
you blew us all away they said
I was going for a floating dandelion wish
but dropped a bomb instead
when the dust settled there I was
conversioned into a pretty bouquet of dead things

in my 20s **true love** looked like
a hot mess of sex in an unlit room of empty sorrys
he's sorry
there were so many other women
she's sorry
for wanting to move in after our first kiss
I'm sorry
for ghosting them
all of our faces were turned away and
I didn't want to search for their suns
through a fog of regret
it's scary to put down roots
if you don't know
where you'll land

I looked up the science of that sunflower meme
is it true
sunflowers are better at love than people
botanists everywhere agree
sunflowers do not
in fact
find each other's face if there's no sun
and my heart let out the bitter laugh
of prophets

but wait
the science said
sunflowers can still teach us a lot
about **true love**
when they are young
they follow the path of the sun across the sky
starstruck
even on cloudy days
as they mature
they stop trailing solar breadcrumbs
content to soak up whatever shines upon them

something in those facts
felt like the kind of truth that's only possible
through the experience of time
nearly 4 decades in
and I've learned how much a person can grow
when they stop trying to force light
from a source with no intention of seeing you blossom
and I've learned that if protected and secured
even dead petals can stir joy
when pressed into poetry
coaxed to bloom with the turn of a page
and I've learned **true love** apologizes
by changing its behavior
roots don't grow in just one direction

did you know
sunflowers that mature into an
ever east-facing direction
attract five times as many pollinators
as those that don't
because blossoms looking east
warm up faster than those facing west

and as I build this life
holding an Ojibwe soul in one hand
and butterfly wings in the other
I think
now that's **true love**
standing in a field of relatives
our backs to the darkness
and faces forever turned
to the promise of a rising sun
letting our warmth and all we've learned
build community with room to grow

Ohíya Acknowledgements

To my parents, Dalton and Taté Walker: Thank you for always loving me, supporting me, and educating me about the important issues (especially the issues most other parents would have prevented their kids from learning). Thank you for helping me be the best me I can be.

To my grandmas Donna Johnson and Della Martinmaas: Thank you for believing in me, and for giving me the tools I need to follow my creative dreams. To the aunties who surround me with all the love, near and far.

To my two favorite teachers, Karen Charleston and Erika Brush. Thank you for building a compassionate classroom environment—a community, really—where my confidence could grow, and I felt safe enough to share and express what I am most passionate about. To Amber McCrary and Abalone Mountain Press for this mind-blowing opportunity. For all the people in my life who have put in the work to overcome transphobic thoughts, language, and behavior.

And finally, to my Ojibwe and Lakota ancestors. For everything (but especially for the stories, the colors, and the florals). Wópila tánka. Chi-miigwech.

Taté's Acknowledgements

What Ohíya said. They're a tough act to follow, so I'll start with them. Ohíya, I am so thankful you chose me to be your mom, that you trust me with your truest self, and that you were willing to trudge through the sometimes-tedious book-making business with me (writing metaphors is hard; drawing them on deadline is harder-and you nailed that ish). I am in awe of your many talents. This poetry book is better with you in it. My world is better with you in it.

To my partner, Dalton Walker, without whom none of what I accomplish is possible. We're closing in on two decades knowing and loving each other, and I'm eternally grateful for everything you've put up with, challenged, supported, and empowered. Chi-miigwech, babe. I have a lot of poems for and about you but didn't think it was appropriate for Ohíya to illustrate any of them *winks at camera* (You're welcome, Ohíya.)

To my iná, my laugh twin, my punner-in-crime, Della Martinmaas, for always being in my corner, even if I didn't know you were there, and for showing me what a joy life can be when you share the best and worst parts of yourself with the people who care.

And thank you to the aunties and elders who have shared their various wisdoms with me, especially Dr. Craig Howe and the team at the Center for American Indian Research and Native Studies for the many years of staggering generosity shown to Očéti Sakówiŋ artists. Since 2015, CAIRNS has curated educational, culturally based art exhibits that center Lakotan narratives and artworks, including my poetry. Wópila táŋka, Dr. Howe, for never asking me to cut down my epically long poems, for helping me translate Star Wars quotes into Lakota, and gently correcting my horrific pronunciation of Ptesáŋwiŋ.

Shout-outs to the many folks who have inspired or uplifted or motivated me to create: To the many Lakota medicine people and ceremony crews of my teens and 20s for showing me how to be a better relative to myself and others; to three of my favorite poets—Tenille Campbell, Layli Long Soldier, and Lydia Zulema Martinez Vega—for your invaluable time and generous support of this book; to Chawa Magaña for the edits and the lovely workspace; to the therapists and the psychiatrists; to Michelle Malach at Fort Lewis College and all the queer stuff we studied; to my high school AP English teacher who shamed me in front of the whole class for writing a poem the wrong way (#stillmad); to my bosom buddy for life, Julia Tasuil; to my high school journalism teacher Jennifer Montgomery and my favorite editor Peter Salter for gifting me writing skills I still use today (not here, obvi); to Jaclyn Roessel, the first person to invite me to read my poetry aloud in front of a live audience; to Jamie Utt and Everyday Feminism for making my first blog (remember those?) poem go viral in 2013; to the haters (yes, it's about you); to my work colleagues who had no idea what they were getting into when they came to my poetry readings; and to all the storytellers baring their souls for the rest of us to connect with and learn from.

And of course, ahéhee' to Amber McCrary and Abalone Mountain Press. The Diné really do make the best Indian tacos (and now the best poetry books—ayyyeee!).

Previous Publications

South Dakota in Poems (2020 South Dakota State Poetry
Society Anthology): *Root My Heart at Wounded Knee*

Center for American Indian Research and Native Studies
- *Root My Heart at Wounded Knee* (Takuwe exhibit,
  March 2018)

- *For Tapúŋ Sá Wiŋ* (Tapun Sa Win exhibit, April
  2017)

- *Critical Remembrance* (Articles of a Treaty
  exhibit, May 2019)

- *Lakota Ouroboros* (The Great Race exhibit, March
  2016)

- *From Ptesáŋwiŋ, With Love* (The Gift exhibit,
  2021)

ANMLY (July 2020)
- *I Like Tacos*
- *The Darkest Everything*
- *Viral Aspirations: A Love Story*

About the Author

Taté Walker (they/them) is a Lakota citizen of the Cheyenne River Sioux Tribe of South Dakota. They are an award-winning Two Spirit storyteller living in Arizona. Learn more at jtatewalker.com.

About the Illustrator

Ohíya Walker (they/them) is a Lakota citizen of the Cheyenne River Sioux Tribe and is also Red Lake Ojibwe and Mvskoke Creek. They are an award-winning 13-year-old trans/nonbinary painter and graphic artist combining contemporary and traditional imagery and mediums.

CPSIA information can be obtained
at www.ICGtesting.com
Printed in the USA
LVHW062049090622
720911LV00014B/161